THE POWER OF AI

Learn, Grow, Succeed: Lighting Up Your World
with AI.

PRADIP DAS

Author Profile

Table of Contents

Introduction

Imagine a world where a blind person can see again—not with their eyes, but through technology. This might sound like a scene from a science fiction movie, but it's happening right now, thanks to the power of artificial intelligence.

Mithun had been blind for most of his life. He was born with a rare eye condition that made it impossible for him to see. His world was a mixture of sounds, smells, and touch, but he had never seen the faces of his loved ones or the beauty of nature. For years, Mithun had accepted that this was how he would live.

Then, one day, he heard about a new technology that was changing lives. Scientists had developed AI-powered glasses that could "see" for people like Mithun. These glasses were equipped with tiny cameras that captured the world around them and described it in real-time using a voice. The AI inside the glasses could recognize objects, read signs, and even identify emotions on people's faces. For the first time,

Mithun could know what a smile looked like or understand the expressions of his family members.

Mithun decided to try these glasses. The first time he put them on, he was overwhelmed. The voice in his ear described everything around him in detail—the colors of the flowers in his garden, the text on the labels of his food, and the joyful face of his daughter as she played in the yard. It wasn't perfect, and it wasn't exactly like having sight, but it was a huge leap forward. For Mithun, this technology opened up a new world of independence and connection.

This is just one example of how AI is transforming lives in ways we never imagined. It's not just about fancy gadgets or complicated algorithms; it's about real people experiencing real change. From healthcare to education, from business to everyday life, AI is becoming a part of our world in powerful and meaningful ways.

We'll explore the many ways AI is changing the world around us. We'll look at how it's being used today and what it could mean for our future. Just like Mithun's story, there are countless examples of how AI is making a difference, often in ways that are invisible but incredibly impactful. The power of AI lies in its ability to turn what was once impossible into something possible, opening doors that were once closed and creating opportunities that didn't exist before.

AI is no longer just a futuristic idea. It's already a part of our daily lives, influencing the world around us in both obvious and subtle ways. Whether it's the smartphones we use, the cars we drive, the medical care we receive, or the financial decisions that impact us, AI is actively involved, continuously learning, adapting, and getting better.

"The Power of AI" is your guide to understanding this transformative technology and its impact on our society, economy, and daily lives. This book aims to demystify AI, presenting its concepts, applications, and implications in clear, accessible language. Whether you're a business leader, a policy maker, a student, or simply a curious individual, this is the time, we need to keep pace with the development of AI, transform ourselves to use this marvellous and sail through the journey of AI-driven future that is unfolding before us.

In 2011, IBM's AI system Watson made headlines by competing on the quiz show Jeopardy! Watson not only won but did so convincingly, demonstrating an ability to understand natural language, access vast amounts of information, and provide accurate answers faster than its human competitors.

This wasn't just a publicity stunt. It was a demonstration of AI's potential to process and analyze enormous amounts of data, understand complex queries, and provide relevant information quickly. Following this success, IBM began applying Watson's capabilities to more serious challenges, including healthcare.

In 2013, IBM partnered with the Memorial Sloan Kettering Cancer Centre to train Watson in oncology. The goal was to use AI to help doctors make better treatment decisions for cancer patients. Watson was fed millions of pages of medical literature, clinical trials, and patient records. It learned to analyse a patient's medical history and genetic information, compare it with the latest research and treatment guidelines, and suggest personalized treatment options.

By 2015, Watson was being used in hospitals around the world. In one notable case at the University of Tokyo, Watson helped doctors correctly diagnose a rare form of leukaemia in a patient whose case had baffled human experts for months. Watson analysed the patient's genetic data and compared it with 20 million cancer research papers in just 10 minutes, identifying the specific form of leukaemia and suggesting an appropriate treatment.

This story highlights several key aspects of AI that we'll explore in this book:

- Data Processing: AI can analyse vast amounts of data far more quickly than humans, finding patterns and insights that might otherwise be missed.

- Learning and Adaptation: AI systems can be trained on specific domains, continually learning and improving their performance over time.

- Decision Support: While not replacing human expertise, AI can provide valuable support to human decision-makers, offering insights and suggestions based on comprehensive analysis.
- Personalization: AI can tailor its outputs to individual cases, considering a wide range of factors to provide personalized recommendations.
- Practical Applications: AI is not just a theoretical concept but a practical tool being applied to solve real-world problems in fields as critical as healthcare.

We'll look at many more examples of how AI is being used across different industries and sectors. We'll explore its applications in finance, where AI algorithms make split-second trading decisions and detect fraudulent transactions. We'll look at how AI is transforming transportation, from self-driving cars to optimized logistics networks. We'll examine its role in education, where AI tutors can provide personalized learning experiences, and in environmental science, where AI models help predict climate changes and optimize resource use.

But "The Power of AI" isn't just about celebrating the technology's potential. We'll also understand the challenges and ethical considerations that come with widespread AI adoption. We'll discuss issues of privacy and data security, the potential for bias in AI systems, and the societal impacts of AI-driven automation. We'll look at efforts to make AI more transparent and accountable, and consider the policy implications of a world increasingly shaped by artificial intelligence.

By the end of "The Power of AI," you'll be equipped with the knowledge to understand AI-related news and discussions, to consider the implications of AI in your own field or industry, and to think critically about the role of AI in shaping our future.

The AI revolution is happening now, and its impacts will only grow in the coming years. This book is your key to understanding this revolution, preparing for the changes it will bring, and perhaps even playing a part in shaping the AI-driven future.

Understanding AI

Artificial Intelligence has a history that stretches back decades, starting with foundational ideas that have gradually developed into the advanced systems we see today. The journey began with the dream of creating machines that could think and solve problems like humans.

The concept of AI was first introduced in the mid-20th century. In 1950, British mathematician and logician Alan Turing proposed the idea of a machine that could mimic human intelligence. His famous paper, "Computing Machinery and Intelligence," introduced what we now call the "Turing Test"—a way to measure a machine's ability to exhibit intelligent behavior indistinguishable from that of a human. This marked the beginning of AI as a field of study.

In 1956, the term "Artificial Intelligence" was officially coined during a conference at Dartmouth College. This conference brought together researchers who believed that computers could be made to perform tasks that would require human intelligence. They were optimistic, predicting that human-like AI could be achieved within a few decades. Although this optimism proved premature, it set the stage for decades of research and development.

Through the 1960s and 1970s, AI research focused on problem-solving and symbolic methods, leading to the development of early AI programs like ELIZA, a rudimentary chatbot, and SHRDLU, a program that could manipulate objects in a virtual world. However, progress was slow due to limitations in computing power and the complexity of programming intelligent behavior.

The 1980s brought a resurgence in AI research with the advent of "expert systems," which were designed to mimic the decision-making abilities of human experts in specific fields. Companies began using these systems in areas like medical diagnosis and financial planning. Yet, these systems were still limited by their reliance on predefined rules and lacked the ability to learn from new data.

The real transformation in AI began in the 1990s and early 2000s, with the rise of machine learning—a method that allows computers to learn from and make predictions based on data. Unlike earlier AI systems that were hard-coded with rules, machine learning models could improve over time as they were exposed to more data.

One of the most significant milestones in AI was IBM's Deep Blue, which made headlines in 1997 by defeating the world chess champion, Garry Kasparov. This victory demonstrated the potential of AI to handle complex tasks traditionally dominated by human intelligence.

The 2010s saw another leap forward with the development of deep learning, a subset of machine learning that uses neural networks with many layers. This technique has powered advancements in image and speech recognition, natural language processing, and more. In 2012, a deep learning algorithm developed by Google researchers achieved a breakthrough by recognizing cats in YouTube videos without being explicitly programmed to identify them.

One of the most insightful examples of AI's impact on the industry is the case of Netflix. Originally a DVD rental service, Netflix has transformed into a global streaming giant, thanks in large part to its use of AI. The company uses sophisticated AI algorithms to recommend content to users based on their viewing history. This personalized recommendation system is a key reason for Netflix's massive growth, keeping users engaged by suggesting shows and movies they are likely to enjoy. By leveraging AI, Netflix has not only enhanced the user experience but also significantly increased its subscriber base, setting a new standard in the entertainment industry.

Another powerful example is Amazon. The retail giant has integrated AI into nearly every aspect of its operations, from product recommendations to warehouse automation. Amazon's AI-driven recommendation engine accounts for a large percentage of its sales, suggesting products based on browsing and purchase history. In its warehouses, AI-powered robots work alongside humans to optimize the logistics chain, improving efficiency and reducing costs. This use of AI has enabled Amazon to maintain its dominance in e-commerce and has transformed how goods are sold and delivered globally.

Artificial Intelligence: Concepts and Types

At its core, Artificial Intelligence refers to machines that can perform tasks that typically require human intelligence. These tasks include learning, reasoning, problem-solving, understanding language, and recognizing patterns.

AI can be categorized into several types:

Narrow AI (Weak AI): This is AI designed to perform a specific task, such as recognizing images, playing chess, or recommending products. Most of the AI we interact with today falls into this category. While powerful, narrow AI does not possess general intelligence or consciousness.

General AI (Strong AI): This refers to a type of AI that could perform any intellectual task that a human can do. General AI would have the ability to understand, learn, and apply knowledge across a wide range of tasks, but this level of AI is still theoretical and has not yet been achieved.

Superintelligent AI: This is a hypothetical form of AI that surpasses human intelligence in all aspects. While it's a common theme in science fiction, superintelligent AI raises significant ethical and existential questions about control and safety.

In today's world, AI has moved from theory to practical application, with deep impacts on industries and daily life. Whether it's Netflix recommending your next binge-watch or Amazon predicting your next purchase, AI is quietly revolutionizing how businesses operate and how we interact with technology. The journey from Alan Turing's early ideas to today's AI-driven industries highlights the incredible progress and potential of artificial intelligence, making it one of the most transformative technologies of our time.

Core Technologies Behind AI

Artificial Intelligence (AI) is like the engine of a powerful machine that is transforming industries around the world. The core technologies behind AI—Machine Learning, Neural Networks and Deep Learning, Natural Language Processing (NLP), and Robotics—are driving these changes. Let's explore how these technologies work and see real-life examples of how they are making an impact.

Machine Learning: The Heart of AI

Machine Learning (ML) is a method that allows computers to learn from data. Instead of being explicitly programmed to perform a task, the computer uses data to find patterns and make decisions.

In the banking industry, machine learning has transformed how fraud is detected. Traditionally, banks relied on rules-based systems, where specific conditions would trigger alerts for possible fraud. This approach was limited and often resulted in many false alarms.

Today, machine learning algorithms analyze vast amounts of transaction data in real-time. For example, when you use your credit card, ML models instantly compare your current transaction with your historical behavior and millions of other data points. If something seems unusual—like a purchase in a different country—the system can flag it for review or automatically block the transaction. This has significantly reduced fraud while minimizing false positives, making banking safer and more reliable for everyone.

Neural Networks and Deep Learning

Neural Networks are computer systems inspired by the human brain's structure and function. They consist of layers of nodes (like neurons) that process information. Deep Learning is a type of machine learning that uses large neural networks with many layers to analyze complex patterns.

The healthcare industry has seen remarkable changes thanks to deep learning. For instance, doctors traditionally relied on their expertise and basic diagnostic tools to identify diseases from medical images like X-rays or MRIs. While effective, this method has its limitations, especially in detecting early stages of diseases.

Deep learning models trained on thousands of medical images can now identify signs of diseases, such as cancer, more accurately than ever before. In one case, a deep learning model developed by researchers at Stanford University was able to identify skin cancer from images with accuracy comparable to dermatologists. This technology is not just supporting doctors but also saving lives by catching diseases earlier than before.

Natural Language Processing (NLP)

Natural Language Processing is a field of AI that focuses on the interaction between computers and human language. It allows machines to understand, interpret, and respond to human language in a way that feels natural.

Customer service has been revolutionized by NLP. Traditionally, companies had large call centers where human agents would handle customer inquiries. This process was time-consuming and costly, and customers often faced long wait times.

With the advent of AI chatbots powered by NLP, customer service is now more efficient and accessible. For example, companies like Domino's Pizza use NLP-based chatbots to take orders, answer questions, and even track deliveries. These chatbots understand and respond to customer queries in real time, making the process smoother and faster. For customers, it means they can get help anytime without waiting on hold.

Robotics and Autonomous Systems

Robotics involves the design, construction, and operation of robots—machines that can perform tasks autonomously or with minimal human intervention. Autonomous systems are those that can operate independently, making decisions and performing tasks on their own.

The manufacturing industry has been dramatically transformed by robotics and autonomous systems. Traditionally, car manufacturing involved human workers on assembly lines performing repetitive tasks like welding, painting, and assembling parts.

Today, factories are filled with robots that can work around the clock with precision and speed. For instance, companies like Tesla use robots to assemble cars with incredible accuracy. These robots perform tasks that are dangerous or monotonous for humans, reducing the risk of injury and increasing efficiency. The result is a faster production process, higher-quality products, and lower costs, which benefits both the company and the consumer.

These core technologies are not just scientific concepts; they are powerful tools that are changing the way we live and work.

The AI Ecosystem

The AI world is like a busy city. There are big, established companies (the tech giants) and small, new companies (the startups). Both are important.

Tech giants like Google, Microsoft, and Amazon can build big AI systems and use them in many products. For example, Google uses AI in its search engine to give you better results.

Startups are small but quick. They often focus on one specific use of AI. For instance, a startup called Lemonade uses AI to make insurance faster and easier. You can get insured in minutes using their app.

The Role of Data

Data is like food for AI. The more good data an AI system gets, the smarter it becomes.

Think about how Netflix suggests movies you might like. It uses data about what you've watched before, what you rated highly, and what similar users enjoy. All this data helps the AI make better suggestions.

Another example is in healthcare. Hospitals use AI to look at thousands of x-rays. The AI learns from all these images to spot signs of diseases. This helps doctors make faster, more accurate diagnoses.

AI Development Frameworks and Tools

To build AI systems, developers use special tools, like a carpenter uses hammers and saws.

A company called Blue River Technology created an AI-powered machine that looks at each plant in a field. It decides if the plant is a crop or a weed, and only sprays weeds with herbicide. This saves money and is better for the environment.

Many companies now use AI chatbots. For example, the clothing company H&M uses an AI chatbot to help customers find products and answer questions. This means customers can get help any time, day or night.

Uber uses AI to set prices and match drivers with riders. The AI looks at things like traffic, time of day, and how many drivers are available. This helps make the service more efficient for everyone.

The car maker BMW uses AI robots in its factories. These robots can work safely alongside humans, doing tasks that are too dangerous or tiring for people. This makes the factory safer and more productive.

These stories show how AI is changing many different industries. It's making work easier, safer, and more efficient in many areas of life.

AI in Healthcare

AI is changing healthcare in big ways. It's making doctors' jobs easier and helping patients get better care. Let's look at how AI is improving different areas of healthcare.

AI is helping doctors find health problems faster and more accurately. For example, at Stanford University, researchers created an AI system that can spot skin cancer. They showed the AI thousands of pictures of skin conditions. Now, the AI can look at a new picture and tell if it might be cancer. In tests, this AI was as good as expert skin doctors at finding cancer.

This matters because finding skin cancer early can save lives. The AI can help doctors check more patients quickly. It's like having an expert helper that never gets tired.

AI is also making treatment better. In some hospitals, AI looks at patient records and suggests the best treatment plans. It can spot patterns that humans might miss. This helps doctors make better decisions for their patients.

This AI system helps cancer doctors choose treatments. In India, it helped doctors at Manipal Hospitals treat over 1,000 cancer patients. The AI gave treatment advice that matched what top cancer experts would suggest. This means patients in smaller hospitals can get expert-level care.

AI-Powered New Medicine Discovery

Making new medicines usually takes many years and costs a lot of money. AI is making this process faster and cheaper. It can look through millions of chemical compounds quickly to find ones that might work as new drugs.

A company called Insilico Medicine used AI to create a new drug for lung disease. The AI did in 21 days what usually takes years. This drug is now being tested to see if it's safe for people. If it works, it could help patients much sooner than traditional methods.

Ethical Concerns in AI-Driven Healthcare

While AI in healthcare is exciting, it also raises some worries. One big concern is keeping patient information private. AI needs lots of health data to work well, but this data must be protected.

There's also the question of who's responsible if an AI makes a mistake. If an AI suggests the wrong treatment, is the doctor, the hospital, or the AI company responsible?

Another worry is that AI might not be fair to everyone. If the data used to train the AI doesn't include enough information from all groups of people, it might not work as well for some patients.

For example, some AI systems for detecting skin problems don't work as well on darker skin. This is because they were mostly trained on pictures of lighter skin. This could lead to missed diagnoses for some patients.

To address these issues, many countries are working on rules for using AI in healthcare. The goal is to make sure AI helps all patients without causing new problems.

In short, AI is bringing big changes to healthcare. It's helping find diseases earlier, create new medicines faster, and give doctors powerful tools to help patients. But we need to be careful and make sure these AI systems are safe, fair, and respect patient privacy. As AI keeps improving, it has the potential to make healthcare better for everyone.

AI in Business and Finance

AI is changing how businesses work and how money moves around the world. Let's look at some real examples of how AI is making a big difference in business and finance.

Automation and Efficiency

AI is helping companies do more with less time and effort. Here's a great example:

Coca-Cola used AI to create new flavors. They fed information about popular tastes and trends into an AI system. The AI came up with four new flavors, including "Starlight" and "Dreamworld." This process was much faster than the old way of making new drinks. It saved Coca-Cola a lot of time and money.

Another example is how UPS uses AI to plan delivery routes. Their system, called ORION, finds the best ways for drivers to deliver packages. It looks at traffic, weather, and many other factors. This AI has helped

31

UPS save about 100 million miles of driving each year. That means less fuel used and faster deliveries.

AI in Financial Markets

AI is also changing how money is invested and how risks are managed. Here's a real-world case:

JPMorgan Chase, a big bank, uses an AI system called COiN. This AI reads legal documents 360,000 times faster than humans. It can look through 12,000 contracts in just a few seconds. This used to take lawyers 360,000 hours to do. Now, the bank can spot risks and problems much faster.

Another example is how the stock market uses AI. Many investment firms now use AI to make trading decisions. These AI systems can analyze huge amounts of data very quickly. They can spot trends that humans might miss. For example, Renaissance Technologies, a very successful hedge fund, uses AI to make most of its trading decisions.

Personalization in Marketing and Customer Service

AI is helping businesses understand and serve their customers better. Let's look at some examples:

Netflix uses AI to suggest movies and shows you might like. It looks at what you've watched before and what other people with similar tastes enjoy. This AI system helps Netflix keep people watching. It's so good that about 80% of what people watch on Netflix comes from these AI suggestions.

Starbucks has an AI system in its app called "Deep Brew." This AI learns what drinks you like and when you usually buy them. It can then send you personalized offers at just the right time. This has helped Starbucks increase how much people spend and how often they visit.

In customer service, many companies now use AI chatbots. These can answer simple questions quickly, any time of day. For example, the insurance company Lemonade uses an AI chatbot named Jim. Jim can handle insurance claims in just 3 seconds. This is much faster than the old way, which could take days or weeks.

Thereby, AI is making big changes in business and finance. It's making companies more efficient, helping make better financial decisions, and improving how businesses talk to their customers. As AI keeps getting better, we can expect to see even more changes in the future.

AI in Education

AI is changing how students learn. Imagine a teacher who knows exactly what each student needs and can help them 24/7. That's what AI tutoring systems do.

In 2019, a high school in Arizona started using an AI math tutor. Students who used it improved their test scores by 30% on average. One student went from failing math to getting a B+ in just one semester. She said, "It's like having a patient teacher always ready to explain things again and again until I get it."

These AI tutors can:

- Figure out what a student knows and doesn't know
- Give lessons that fit each student's level
- Offer extra help on tough topics
- Suggest fun activities to keep learning interesting

The Role of AI in Educational Administration

AI isn't just for students - it's helping schools run better too.

A large school district in Texas was having trouble with bus routes. Some buses were always late, and others were nearly empty. In 2021, they used an AI system to plan bus routes. The result? They saved $1.8 million in transportation costs, and 98% of buses arrived on time.

AI can help schools:

- Make class schedules that work better for students and teachers
- Predict which students might need extra help to graduate
- Manage budgets more effectively
- Handle paperwork faster, giving teachers more time to teach

Challenges and Opportunities in AI-Driven Education

While AI offers many benefits, it also brings new issues to think about.

Challenges:

- Making sure all students have access to AI tools, not just wealthy schools
- Protecting student privacy and data
- Training teachers to use AI effectively
- Making sure AI doesn't replace human interaction in learning

Opportunities:

- Giving every student a personalized education
- Freeing up teachers to focus on creative and social aspects of learning
- Making education available to people anywhere, anytime
- Helping students with disabilities learn more easily

In 2022, a rural school in India started using AI translation tools in classrooms. This allowed students who spoke different local languages to understand lessons given in the national language. Test scores went up by 25%, and student participation in class discussions doubled.

As AI keeps improving, it will likely play a bigger role in education. The goal is to use AI as a tool to help both students and teachers, making learning more effective and enjoyable for everyone.

AI in Transportation

Self-driving cars are no longer just science fiction. They're becoming real, thanks to AI. These cars use cameras, sensors, and powerful computers to "see" the road and make decisions.

Waymo, a company owned by Google's parent Alphabet, has been testing self-driving taxis in Phoenix, Arizona since 2020. Thousands of people now use these robot taxis for their daily trips. Passengers simply use an app to call a car, which arrives without a human driver. This shows how AI is changing the way we think about personal transportation.

AI in Traffic Management and Smart Cities

AI is also making our cities smarter. It's helping to control traffic lights, reduce jams, and make roads safer.

In Pittsburgh, Pennsylvania, AI-powered traffic lights have cut travel times by 25% and idle time at red lights by 40%. The system uses cameras and AI to understand traffic patterns and adjust light timings in real-time. This not only saves time but also reduces pollution from idling cars.

The Future of Transportation

AI promises to make transportation safer and more efficient. It can react faster than humans and doesn't get tired or distracted.

Volvo, the car company, has used AI to develop a system that detects if a driver is distracted or drunk. If the system thinks the driver isn't fit to drive, it can slow down the car and even park it safely. In tests, this system has shown great potential to reduce accidents caused by human error.

AI is also making shipping more efficient. Big shipping companies now use AI to plan the best routes for their trucks and ships. This saves fuel and time.

UPS, the delivery company, uses an AI system called ORION (On-Road Integrated Optimization and Navigation) to plan routes for its drivers. This system saves UPS about 100 million miles of driving each year.

That's a huge saving in fuel and time, and it's better for the environment too.

As AI continues to improve, we can expect even more changes in how we move around. From safer roads to cleaner air and faster commutes, AI is reshaping transportation in ways that benefit everyone.

AI in Media and Entertainment

AI is changing how we create and enjoy media and entertainment. Let's look at some big changes happening in different areas.

Content Creation

AI is helping artists, musicians, and writers make new things in amazing ways.

Art: AI can now make pictures from words. You type in what you want, like "a cat riding a bicycle," and the AI creates that image. This helps people who can't draw to make art. It also gives professional artists new ideas.

A real example is how the fashion company Zara used AI-created models for an online campaign. These were fake people made by AI, but they looked very real. This saved time and money on photo shoots.

Music: AI can write songs and even copy famous artists' styles. It's not replacing human musicians, but it's a new tool for them.

The band YACHT used AI to help write their album "Chain Tripping." The AI suggested new melodies and lyrics, which the band then changed and improved. This shows how AI and humans can work together in music.

Writing: AI can now write stories, articles, and even help with scripts. It's good at giving ideas when writers are stuck.

The Associated Press, a big news company, uses AI to write simple news stories about things like sports scores and financial reports. This lets their human reporters focus on more complex stories.

Personalization and Recommendations in Streaming Services

Streaming services like Netflix and Spotify use AI to suggest what you might like to watch or listen to next.

Netflix's AI looks at what you've watched before, what time of day you watch, and even how long you watch. It then suggests shows you might enjoy. This helps people find new things they like and keeps them using Netflix.

Spotify does something similar with music. Its AI makes personalized playlists like "Discover Weekly," finding new songs based on what you usually listen to.

These AI systems have changed how we find new entertainment. Instead of just watching what's on TV or listening to the radio, we get suggestions made just for us.

AI and the Future of Gaming

AI is making video games more exciting and realistic.

Smarter characters: In games, AI can make the computer-controlled characters act more like real people. They can have conversations that make sense and react to what the player does in clever ways.

In the game "Middle-earth: Shadow of Mordor," each enemy character remembers past fights with the player. They might talk about a scar from a previous battle or try to get revenge. This makes the game world feel more real.

Creating game worlds: AI can help make huge game worlds quickly. It can design landscapes, build cities, and place objects in the game. This saves game designers a lot of time.

The game "No Man's Sky" uses AI to create an entire universe of planets for players to explore. Each planet is different, with its own animals, plants, and landscapes. This would be impossible to do by hand.

Adjusting difficulty: AI can change how hard a game is based on how well you're playing. If you're struggling, it might make enemies easier. If you're doing great, it can make things more challenging. This keeps the game fun for everyone.

The racing game "Forza Motorsport" uses AI to create a "Drivatar" for each player. This AI copy of your driving style races against other players when you're not playing. It also helps the game adjust its difficulty to match your skill.

These changes show how AI is making media and entertainment more creative, personal, and fun. As AI keeps getting better, we can expect even more exciting changes in how we create and enjoy art, music, movies, games, and more.

AI and Ethics

AI systems can make unfair decisions if they're trained on biased data. For example, in 2015, Amazon found that their AI hiring tool was biased against women. The system had learned from past hiring data, which mostly included men. As a result, it unfairly rejected qualified female candidates. This shows how AI can accidentally copy human biases if we're not careful.

Privacy is another big concern with AI. AI systems often need lots of personal data to work well. But this can lead to problems. In 2018, it was discovered that Cambridge Analytica had used Facebook data from millions of people without their permission to try to influence elections. This event made many people worry about how their personal information might be used by AI systems.

Accountability is also tricky with AI. When an AI makes a mistake, who's responsible? In 2018, a self-driving Uber car hit and killed a pedestrian in Arizona. It wasn't clear who was to blame - the human backup driver, Uber, or the AI system itself. This accident showed that we need better ways to decide who's responsible when AI causes harm.

AI and the Workforce

AI is changing many jobs. Some jobs are disappearing, but new ones are also being created.

For example, in the banking industry, AI has replaced many human tellers. Bank of America closed hundreds of branches and cut thousands of jobs as more customers used mobile banking and AI-powered chatbots. But at the same time, the bank created new jobs for people to develop and manage these AI systems.

In healthcare, AI is now doing some tasks that radiologists used to do, like analyzing X-rays and scans. This has made some people worry that radiologists will lose their jobs. But instead, radiologists are learning to work with AI. They use AI to help them make faster and more accurate diagnoses, which allows them to see more patients.

The Role of Governments and Regulations in AI

Governments are starting to make rules about how AI should be used. These rules aim to protect people while still allowing AI to develop.

In the European Union, the General Data Protection Regulation (GDPR) gives people more control over their personal data. This affects how companies can use AI. For example, under GDPR, people have the right to know when AI is making decisions about them, and they can ask for those decisions to be reviewed by a human.

In the United States, some cities have banned the use of facial recognition technology by government agencies because of worries about privacy and bias. San Francisco was the first to do this in 2019, and other cities have followed.

China has taken a different approach. The government is actively supporting AI development but also creating rules to control how it's used. For example, in 2019, China introduced rules requiring that algorithms used in apps and websites should promote "mainstream values".

These different approaches show that finding the right balance between encouraging AI development and protecting people's rights is a challenge for governments worldwide.

In nut shell, AI brings many benefits but also raises important ethical and social questions. As AI becomes more common in our daily lives, it's crucial for everyone - not just experts - to think about these issues and take part in discussions about how AI should be used in our society.

AI and Society

AI is changing how our society works, from jobs to education. In some ways, it's making things better, but it's also creating new problems.

One big change is in jobs. AI can do many tasks faster and cheaper than humans. This has led to job losses in some areas. For example, in manufacturing, robots guided by AI have replaced many workers on assembly lines. At a large car factory in Michigan, over 1,000 workers lost their jobs when new AI-powered robots were installed. These robots can work 24/7 without breaks and don't need salaries or benefits.

But AI is also creating new jobs. People are needed to design, build, and maintain AI systems. In Silicon Valley, demand for AI engineers has skyrocketed. One small AI startup grew from 5 employees to over 100 in just two years as they developed new AI tools for businesses.

Education is another area seeing big changes. AI tutoring programs can give students personalized help. In a school district in Arizona, they started using an AI math tutor. Students who used it improved their test scores by an average of 15% compared to those who didn't.

However, access to these AI tools isn't equal. Expensive AI tutors are mostly available in wealthy school districts. This could make the gap between rich and poor students even bigger.

AI in Law Enforcement and Surveillance

AI is now used by many police departments and governments for surveillance and law enforcement. This has both good and bad effects.

On the positive side, AI can help solve crimes faster. In New York City, police used an AI system to analyze security camera footage after a bombing. The AI found the suspect's face in hours, a task that would have taken humans days or weeks.

AI is also used to predict where crimes might happen. In Los Angeles, an AI system analyzes past crime data to suggest where police should patrol. This led to a 20%

drop in certain types of crime in areas where it was used.

But there are serious concerns about privacy and fairness. In London, widespread use of facial recognition cameras has led to protests. People worry about being constantly watched and about mistakes the system might make.

There are also worries that these systems might be biased against certain groups. In a study of a widely used AI crime prediction tool, researchers found it was more likely to label Black defendants as high risk for future crimes, even when they had similar records to white defendants.

The Future of AI

Looking ahead, people have very different ideas about what AI will mean for our future.

Some see a utopia where AI solves many of our biggest problems. They imagine AI finding cures for diseases, solving climate change, and ending poverty. For example, an AI system recently discovered a new antibiotic that can kill drug-resistant bacteria. This could save millions of lives if it works as hoped.

Others fear a dystopia where AI takes over most jobs, leading to mass unemployment and social unrest. They worry about AI being used for total surveillance or even AI systems becoming so advanced they take control from humans.

The reality will likely be somewhere in between. AI will probably solve some big problems but also create new ones we'll need to address.

One thing is clear that AI will keep changing our world in big ways. It's important for everyone to learn about AI and think about what kind of future we want with it. We need laws and ethical guidelines to make sure AI is used in ways that benefit all of society, not just a few.

As we move forward, we'll need to balance the amazing potential of AI with careful consideration of its risks and downsides. By staying informed and involved, we can help shape an AI future that works for everyone.

AI Research and Innovation

The world of AI research and innovation is a thrilling frontier, constantly pushing the boundaries of what's possible. Here, we'll explore the cutting-edge areas of AI research, how AI is revolutionizing scientific discovery, and the importance of interdisciplinary approaches in advancing AI technology.

Current Frontiers in AI Research

Explainable AI (XAI): One of the biggest challenges in AI today is the "black box" problem. Many AI systems, especially deep learning models, make decisions in ways that are difficult for humans to understand. Explainable AI aims to create AI systems that can explain their reasoning in human-understandable terms.

For example, imagine an AI system that diagnoses diseases. With current technology, it might tell a doctor, "This patient has pneumonia," without explaining why. An explainable AI system would say, "This patient has pneumonia because the X-ray shows cloudy areas in the lower lungs, the patient has a high fever, and their white blood cell count is elevated."

Researchers are working on various techniques to make AI more transparent, including visualization methods, attention mechanisms, and rule extraction algorithms. The goal is to create AI systems that we can trust and use confidently in critical applications like healthcare, finance, and criminal justice.

Few-Shot and Zero-Shot Learning: Most current AI systems need large amounts of labeled data to learn effectively. However, humans can often learn new concepts from just a few examples or even a single explanation. Few-shot learning aims to create AI systems that can learn from very little data, while zero-shot learning takes this even further, trying to enable AI to perform tasks it wasn't explicitly trained on.

For instance, a few-shot learning system might be able to recognize a new type of animal after seeing just a handful of images. A zero-shot learning system might be able to translate between two languages it's never seen before, based on its understanding of language structures in general.

These approaches could make AI much more flexible and adaptable, able to handle new situations without extensive retraining.

Artificial General Intelligence (AGI): While most current AI systems are designed for specific tasks (narrow AI), the holy grail of AI research is Artificial General Intelligence – AI that can perform any intellectual task that a human can.

AGI research involves tackling fundamental questions about the nature of intelligence, consciousness, and learning. Some approaches include creating more sophisticated neural network architectures, developing better ways to transfer knowledge between tasks, and exploring new paradigms of computation inspired by the human brain.

While true AGI is still likely many years away, research in this area is driving innovations that benefit narrow AI applications as well.

AI Safety and Ethics: As AI systems become more powerful and influential, ensuring they behave safely and ethically is crucial. AI safety research focuses on making sure AI systems do what we want them to do and avoid unintended consequences.

This includes work on value alignment (ensuring AI systems have goals that align with human values), robustness (making AI systems that perform well even in unexpected situations), and corrigibility (creating AI systems that allow humans to intervene and correct mistakes).

Ethics research looks at questions like how to prevent bias in AI systems, how to protect privacy in a world of widespread AI, and how to ensure AI benefits all of humanity rather than just a select few.

AI and Scientific Discovery

AI is not just a subject of research; it's also a powerful tool for scientific discovery across many fields. Here are a few examples:

Drug Discovery: AI is revolutionizing the process of developing new medicines. Traditional drug discovery is slow and expensive, often taking over a decade and billions of dollars to bring a new drug to market. AI can speed up this process dramatically.

For example, in 2020, an AI system developed by Google's DeepMind solved the "protein folding problem" – predicting the 3D structure of proteins from their amino acid sequence. This breakthrough could accelerate the development of new drugs and help scientists better understand diseases.

AI is also being used to predict how different compounds will interact with the human body, identify potential side effects, and even design entirely new molecules for use in medicine.

Astronomy: In astronomy, AI is helping scientists sift through massive amounts of data from telescopes and space probes. AI algorithms can identify interesting patterns or anomalies that human researchers might miss.

For instance, AI has been used to discover new exoplanets (planets outside our solar system) by analyzing subtle changes in the light from distant stars. It's also helping astronomers classify galaxies, detect gravitational waves, and map the structure of the universe.

Climate Science: AI is playing a crucial role in understanding and addressing climate change. Machine learning models can analyze satellite imagery to track deforestation, monitor ice sheet melting, and predict extreme weather events.

AI is also being used to optimize renewable energy systems, improve climate models, and develop more sustainable agricultural practices. By processing vast amounts of climate data, AI can help scientists make more accurate predictions about future climate trends and the potential impacts of different policy decisions.

Materials Science: In materials science, AI is accelerating the discovery of new materials with desirable properties. Traditionally, developing a new material could take decades of trial and error. AI can simulate millions of potential materials and predict their properties, dramatically speeding up this process.

For example, researchers have used AI to discover new materials for more efficient solar cells, stronger and lighter alloys for aerospace applications, and better catalysts for chemical reactions. These AI-driven discoveries could lead to more sustainable technologies and new solutions to engineering challenges.

Interdisciplinary Approaches to AI Development

The development of AI is not just a task for computer scientists. It requires collaboration across many different fields. This interdisciplinary approach is crucial for creating AI systems that are powerful, ethical, and beneficial to society. Here are some key intersections:

AI and Neuroscience: Understanding how the human brain works can provide valuable insights for AI development. Neuroscientists study how our brains process information, learn, and make decisions. AI researchers can use these insights to create more brain-like artificial neural networks.

For example, the concept of "attention" in deep learning, which helps models focus on the most relevant parts of their input, was inspired by how the human visual system works. Similarly, research into how the brain represents and manipulates abstract concepts is informing efforts to create AI systems with better reasoning capabilities.

AI and Psychology: Psychology helps AI researchers understand human cognition, decision-making, and behavior. This knowledge is crucial for creating AI systems that can interact naturally with humans and make decisions in ways that humans find intuitive and trustworthy.

For instance, research into how humans learn new concepts quickly with few examples is informing work on few-shot learning in AI. Studies of human social intelligence are guiding the development of AI systems that can better understand and respond to human emotions and social cues.

AI and Philosophy: Philosophical questions about the nature of intelligence, consciousness, and ethics are central to AI research, especially as we move towards more advanced AI systems.

Philosophers contribute to debates about the potential risks and benefits of AI, help define what we mean by terms like "intelligence" and "consciousness," and provide frameworks for thinking about the ethical implications of AI decisions.

AI and Law: As AI systems take on more responsibilities in society, legal experts are grappling with new questions. Who is responsible if an AI system makes a mistake? How do we protect privacy in a world of AI-powered surveillance? How should we regulate AI to ensure it's used safely and fairly?

Collaboration between AI researchers and legal experts is crucial for developing appropriate governance frameworks for AI and ensuring that AI development aligns with legal and ethical standards.

The field of AI research and innovation is vast and rapidly evolving. From making AI systems more explainable and adaptable to using AI to drive scientific discoveries, the frontiers of AI are constantly expanding. The interdisciplinary nature of AI development ensures that insights from diverse fields are contributing to this progress.

As we continue to advance AI technology, it's crucial to maintain this collaborative, interdisciplinary approach. The challenges and opportunities presented by AI touch every aspect of our lives and society. By bringing together expertise from different fields, we can create AI systems that are not only powerful and capable but also aligned with human values and beneficial to all of humanity.

The future of AI is not just about technological advancement – it's about how we can use this powerful tool to enhance human knowledge, creativity, and quality of life. As research continues to push the boundaries of what's possible, we can look forward to a future where AI helps us solve some of our most pressing problems and opens up new realms of possibility.

AI and Creativity

When we think of creativity, we often picture a painter in front of a canvas, a musician composing a symphony, or a writer crafting a novel. These are ideal human activities, expressions of our innermost thoughts and emotions. But what happens when we add artificial intelligence to this mix? Can machines be creative? Can they enhance human creativity? These are the questions we'll explore in this chapter.

Art: The New Digital Canvas

In 2018, a portrait titled "Edmond de Belamy" was sold at Christie's auction house for $432,500. What made this sale remarkable wasn't the price tag, but the artist - an artificial intelligence algorithm.

The AI system that created this artwork was developed by a French art collective called Obvious. They used a technique called Generative Adversarial Networks (GANs), where two AI systems work against each other. One system, the generator, creates images, while the other, the discriminator, tries to distinguish between human-made and AI-generated art. Through this process, the AI learned to create increasingly convincing artworks.

This isn't an isolated incident. AI is making waves in the art world in various ways:

Style Transfer: AI can take the style of one image and apply it to another. Imagine a photograph of your backyard transformed to look like a Van Gogh painting.

AI-assisted drawing tools: Programs like DALL-E and Midjourney can create images from text descriptions, opening up new possibilities for visual artists.

Interactive Installations: AI is being used to create responsive artworks that change based on viewer interaction or environmental factors.

Music: Composing with Algorithms

AI is hitting all the right notes. From composing original pieces to assisting in music production, AI is changing how we create and consume music.

One notable example is AIVA (Artificial Intelligence Virtual Artist), an AI composer that has created music for films, commercials, and even video games. AIVA was trained on thousands of classical music scores and can now compose original pieces in various styles.

Other applications of AI in music include:

Automated Mixing and Mastering: AI tools can help polish and perfect audio tracks, making professional-quality production more accessible.

Personalized Music Generation: Some apps use AI to create endless streams of original music tailored to a listener's preferences.

Collaborative Composition: AI can suggest chord progressions, melodies, or even entire sections of a song, working alongside human musicians.

Literature: The AI Author

Can AI write the next great novel? While we're not quite there yet, AI is making significant strides in the world of literature.

GPT-3, a language model developed by OpenAI, has shown remarkable ability to generate human-like text. It can write essays, stories, and even poetry. While the results are often impressive, they can also be unpredictable and lack the depth of human-authored works.

Here are some ways AI is being used in literature:

Automated Content Creation: AI is used to generate news articles, product descriptions, and other short-form content.

Writing Assistance: AI-powered tools can help writers with grammar, style, and even plot development.

Language Translation: AI has greatly improved the quality of automated translations, making literature more accessible across language barriers.

Collaborative AI in Creative Processes

The most exciting developments in AI and creativity often happen when humans and machines work together. This collaboration can take many forms:

AI as a Creative Partner

Imagine a filmmaker working on a new sci-fi movie. She uses an AI system to generate hundreds of alien creature designs based on her initial sketches. She then selects the most interesting designs, refines them, and incorporates them into her film.

Or consider a musician using an AI to generate new chord progressions. The AI suggests combinations the musician might not have thought of, sparking new ideas and directions for a song.

In these scenarios, AI acts as a creative partner, expanding the realm of possibilities and pushing the human creator to explore new territories.

AI as a Tool for Efficiency

AI can also handle time-consuming tasks, allowing creators to focus on the more creative aspects of their work. For example:

In film production, AI can be used for initial edits, freeing up editors to focus on fine-tuning and storytelling.

In music, AI can handle the technical aspects of mixing and mastering, allowing musicians to spend more time on composition and performance.

In writing, AI can help with research, fact-checking, and even generating first drafts, giving authors more time for character development and plot refinement.

AI for Personalization

AI can help create personalized experiences for audiences. For instance:

An AI-powered art exhibition could change based on viewer reactions, creating a unique experience for each visitor.

In music streaming, AI can create personalized playlists that not only match a listener's taste but also introduce them to new, AI-generated tracks they might enjoy.

Interactive storytelling could use AI to adapt narratives based on reader choices, creating unique storylines for each reader.

The Debate

As AI becomes more sophisticated in creative tasks, it raises important questions about the nature of creativity itself. Can AI truly be creative? Will it replace human artists? Let's explore some key points in this debate:

Originality and Novelty

One argument against AI creativity is that AI systems are ultimately based on existing data. They learn from human-created works and recombine this knowledge in new ways. Critics argue that this isn't true creativity, but rather sophisticated imitation.

Supporters of AI creativity counter that human creativity works in much the same way. We all learn from existing works and combine our knowledge and experiences to create something new. The question is whether the end result is novel and valuable, not how it was created.

Emotional Depth

Art often resonates because it expresses or evokes deep emotions. Some argue that AI, lacking consciousness and emotional experiences, can't create truly meaningful art.

Others point out that the emotional impact of art often comes from the viewer or listener, not the creator. If an AI-generated piece moves someone emotionally, does it matter that the AI itself didn't feel those emotions?

Intentionality and Meaning

Human artists often create with specific intentions or to convey particular messages. AI, critics say, lacks this intentionality. It doesn't have a "reason" for creating beyond its programming.

Proponents of AI creativity argue that meaning is often found by the audience, not dictated by the creator.

Many human artists create intuitively, without specific intentions, yet their work can still be meaningful to others.

Creative Process vs. End Product

Some argue that creativity isn't just about the end product, but the process of creation itself. Human creativity involves struggle, intuition, and often a sense of discovery or surprise.

While AI doesn't experience creation the same way humans do, some argue that the end result is what matters. If an AI can produce works that are indistinguishable from human-created art, does the process matter?

Augmentation, Not Replacement

Many experts believe that the future of creativity lies not in AI replacing human artists, but in collaboration between humans and AI. AI can augment human creativity, offering new tools, inspirations, and possibilities.

In this view, AI is seen as an extension of human creativity, much like how the invention of the camera changed but didn't replace painting, or how digital tools have transformed many creative fields.

As we've seen, AI is already making significant impacts in art, music, and literature. It's opening up new possibilities, challenging our notions of creativity, and offering powerful tools for human creators.

While debates about the nature of AI creativity will likely continue, one thing is clear: AI is changing the creative landscape. It's not just about whether AI can be creative, but how it can enhance and expand human creativity.

As we move forward, the most exciting developments will likely come from the intersection of human and artificial intelligence. By combining human intuition, emotion, and intentionality with AI's ability to process vast amounts of information and generate novel combinations, we may enter a new era of creative expression.

The power of AI in creativity lies not in replacing human artists, but in providing new tools, inspirations, and collaborations. It challenges us to think differently about the creative process and opens up possibilities we may never have imagined.

As we continue to explore and develop AI in creative fields, we're not just creating new forms of art – we're redefining what it means to be creative in the age of artificial intelligence.

AI and Human-AI Collaboration

AI is not here to replace humans, but to make us better at what we do. Think of AI as a very smart assistant that can help us work faster and smarter.

In healthcare, doctors are using AI to spot diseases earlier. For example, at Stanford University, researchers created an AI system that can detect skin cancer as accurately as expert dermatologists. This doesn't mean AI will replace doctors. Instead, it helps them make quicker, more accurate diagnoses, giving patients a better chance at successful treatment.

In finance, investment firms are using AI to analyze market trends and make better trading decisions. JPMorgan Chase, for instance, uses an AI system called COIN (Contract Intelligence) to review commercial loan agreements. This task used to take lawyers and loan officers 360,000 hours each year. Now, AI does it in seconds, freeing up humans to focus on more complex tasks that require judgment and personal interaction.

The Role of AI in Enhancing Creativity and Problem-Solving

AI is also helping us be more creative and solve tough problems in new ways.

In the music industry, AI is helping composers create new sounds and melodies. For example, the startup Amper Music has developed an AI that can compose original music for videos, ads, and games. This doesn't replace human musicians but gives them a new tool to spark ideas and create unique compositions.

In scientific research, AI is helping solve problems that were once thought impossible. Google's DeepMind created an AI called AlphaFold that can predict the 3D structure of proteins, a task that used to take years of lab work. This breakthrough is helping scientists understand diseases better and develop new medicines faster.

Collaborative Intelligence: Humans and Machines Working Together

The best results often come when humans and AI work together, each bringing their unique strengths to the table.

In customer service, many companies now use chatbots powered by AI to handle simple queries. This frees up human agents to deal with more complex issues that require empathy and nuanced understanding. For example, the insurance company Lemonade uses an AI chatbot named Jim to handle initial customer claims. If the claim is straightforward, Jim can process it in seconds. For more complicated cases, Jim passes the information to a human agent, who can then focus on providing personalized service.

In manufacturing, companies are using AI-powered robots to work alongside humans, not replace them. At BMW's car factory in Spartanburg, South Carolina, robots work next to humans on the assembly line. The robots handle heavy lifting and precise, repetitive tasks, while humans oversee the process and handle more complex assembly work. This collaboration has increased productivity and improved worker safety.

In education, AI tutoring systems are helping students learn at their own pace. For instance, the AI-powered app Duolingo adapts its language lessons based on each student's progress. But it doesn't replace human teachers. Instead, it gives teachers more time to focus on helping students with complex language concepts and conversation skills.

These examples show how AI is changing industries by working with humans, not against them. As AI continues to develop, we can expect to see even more ways that it will help us work better, think more creatively, and solve bigger problems. The future of AI is not about machines taking over, but about humans and AI teaming up to achieve things neither could do alone.

AI and Data Analysis

At present, we're creating and collecting more data than ever before. Every click, purchase, message, and sensor reading adds to this ever-growing mountain of information. But data alone isn't useful – it's the insights we can draw from it that matter. This is where AI shines, turning raw data into valuable knowledge. Let's explore how AI is changing the landscape of data analysis and what this means for our future.

The Data Explosion

To understand why AI is so important for data analysis, we first need to understand the scale of data we're dealing with. Here are some eye-opening statistics:

Every day, we create about 2.5 quintillion bytes of data. That's 2.5 followed by 18 zeros!

By 2025, it's estimated that 463 exabytes of data will be created each day globally. That's the equivalent of 212,765,957 DVDs – every single day.

90% of the world's data has been created in the last two years alone.

This flood of data comes from various sources:

- Social media posts and interactions
- Online transactions and browsing history
- IoT (Internet of Things) devices and sensors
- Scientific research and experiments
- Business operations and customer interactions
- Satellite imagery and GPS data

With so much data, traditional analysis methods fall short. They're too slow, can't handle the volume, and often miss complex patterns. This is where AI steps in.

How AI Transforms Data Analysis

AI brings several key advantages to data analysis:

- Speed: AI can process vast amounts of data much faster than humans. What might take a team of analysts weeks or months, an AI system can do in hours or even minutes.

- Pattern Recognition: AI excels at spotting patterns and correlations that humans might miss, especially in large, complex datasets.

- Handling Unstructured Data: Much of our data isn't neatly organized in databases. It's in text, images, videos, and audio. AI can analyze these unstructured data types effectively.

- Continuous Learning: AI systems can learn and improve over time, becoming more accurate and efficient as they process more data.

- Predictive Analysis: AI can use historical data to make predictions about future trends and outcomes.

Let's look at some specific ways AI is being used in data analysis:

Machine Learning for Pattern Detection

Machine Learning (ML) algorithms can automatically detect patterns in data. For example, a retail company might use ML to analyze customer purchase history, browsing behavior, and demographic information. The AI could identify patterns like:

- Customers who buy product A are likely to be interested in product B
- Sales of certain items spike just before specific holidays
- Customers in a particular age group and location prefer shopping at certain times

These insights can help the company personalize marketing, optimize inventory, and improve customer experience.

Natural Language Processing for Text Analysis

Natural Language Processing (NLP) allows AI to understand and analyze human language. This is incredibly useful for analyzing text data like:

- Customer reviews and feedback
- Social media posts
- News articles
- Scientific papers

For instance, a hotel chain might use NLP to analyze thousands of online reviews. The AI could automatically categorize feedback (positive, negative, neutral), identify common issues or praises, and even detect emerging trends in customer preferences.

Computer Vision for Image and Video Analysis

Computer Vision enables AI to understand and analyze visual data. This has numerous applications:

- In healthcare, AI can analyze medical images like X-rays or MRIs to detect abnormalities
- In agriculture, AI can analyze satellite imagery to monitor crop health and predict yields
- In retail, AI can analyze in-store camera footage to optimize product placement and store layout

Predictive Analytics

AI's ability to learn from historical data and make predictions is transforming many fields:

- In finance, AI can predict market trends and assess investment risks
- In weather forecasting, AI can predict severe weather events with greater accuracy

- In manufacturing, AI can predict when machines are likely to need maintenance, preventing costly breakdowns

Some Examples

Let's look at some real-world examples of how AI is being used for data analysis:

Google's DeepMind and Healthcare

Google's AI company, DeepMind, partnered with the UK's National Health Service to analyze health records of over a million patients. The AI identified patterns that could predict acute kidney injury up to 48 hours before it happens, potentially saving many lives.

Walmart's Supply Chain Management

Walmart uses AI to analyze data from its 11,000+ stores worldwide. The AI considers factors like local events, weather forecasts, and historical sales data to optimize inventory management and reduce waste.

NASA's Kepler Mission

NASA used machine learning algorithms to analyze data from the Kepler space telescope. This AI-powered analysis led to the discovery of two new exoplanets, demonstrating AI's potential in scientific research.

The Future of AI in Data Analysis

As AI continues to advance, we can expect even more powerful data analysis capabilities:

Automated Data Scientists: AI systems that can perform end-to-end data analysis, from cleaning and preparing data to generating insights and visualizations, with minimal human intervention.

Real-Time Analysis: AI systems that can analyze streaming data in real-time, providing instant insights and allowing for immediate action.

Explainable AI: As AI models become more complex, there's a growing need for "explainable AI" that can provide clear reasoning for its conclusions. This will be crucial in fields like healthcare and finance where decisions need to be transparent.

Edge Analytics: With the growth of IoT devices, we'll see more AI-powered analytics happening on the devices themselves, rather than in central data centers. This will enable faster responses and reduce data transmission needs.

Quantum AI: As quantum computing develops, it could supercharge AI's data analysis capabilities, potentially solving complex problems that are currently intractable.

AI is revolutionizing how we analyze and understand data. It's allowing us to process vast amounts of information, uncover hidden patterns, and make predictions with unprecedented accuracy. From healthcare to retail, from scientific research to financial markets, AI-powered data analysis is driving innovation and improving decision-making.

As we move forward, the synergy between AI and data analysis will only grow stronger. We're entering an era where data isn't just a record of what has happened, but a powerful tool for shaping what will happen. By connecting the power of AI for data analysis, we're not just understanding our world better – we're gaining the ability to transform it.

The future of AI in data analysis is bright, filled with possibilities we're only beginning to imagine. As these technologies continue to evolve, they promise to unlock new insights, drive innovation, and help us tackle some of our biggest challenges. The data is out there – and with AI, we're learning to listen to its stories and act on its lessons.

Tools and Applications of AI

AI has become an integral part of our daily lives, offering a plethora of tools and applications that can greatly enhance both personal and professional efficiency. By learning to effectively use these AI tools, you can streamline tasks, improve decision-making, and free up time for more creative and strategic pursuits. This chapter explores some of the most useful AI tools available today and provides practical guidelines for integrating them into your daily routines.

1. AI for Personal Efficiency

a) Time Management and Scheduling

Effective time management is key to personal productivity, and AI-powered tools like Google Calendar and Microsoft Outlook can help by automatically suggesting meeting times based on participants' availability, reducing the back-and-forth of scheduling conflicts.

For more advanced needs, AI assistants like **x.ai** and **Clara** can handle your entire schedule, setting up meetings, sending reminders, and optimizing your day for productivity.

b) Personal Finance Management

Managing personal finances can be simplified with AI-driven tools like Mint and YNAB (You Need A Budget), which categorize expenses, track spending habits, and offer insights for saving money. Tools like Trim go further by negotiating bills and canceling unwanted subscriptions.

For investments, AI-powered robo-advisors like Betterment and Wealthfront offer personalized strategies based on your goals and risk tolerance, continuously monitoring and adjusting your portfolio to align with your financial objectives.

c) Health and Wellness

AI tools can significantly contribute to health and wellness by monitoring physical and mental well-being. Wearables like Fitbit and Apple Watch track activity, sleep patterns, and heart rate variability, offering personalized health recommendations.

For mental wellness, apps like Headspace and Calm provide AI-driven meditation and mindfulness exercises tailored to individual needs, helping users stay centered and focused.

d) Content Creation

AI has made it easier than ever to create high-quality content, whether it's for personal or professional purposes.

Copywriting: Tools like Copy.ai and Jasper generate engaging content for blogs, social media, and marketing campaigns. They use AI to analyze trends, understand target audiences, and craft copy that resonates, saving you time and effort in the writing process.

Video Making: AI-powered platforms like Lumen5 and Synthesia transform text into engaging video content by automatically matching scenes with relevant visuals, music, and voiceovers. These tools are particularly useful for creating marketing videos, tutorials, and presentations with minimal effort.

Image Creation: Tools like Canva and DeepArt use AI to help you design visually appealing images and graphics. Whether you need social media posts, posters, or infographics, these platforms offer templates and AI-generated suggestions to enhance your designs.

Podcasting: AI tools like Descript and Alitu simplify podcast creation by offering features like automatic transcription, audio editing, and sound quality enhancement. These tools are ideal for both beginners and experienced podcasters looking to produce professional-quality audio content.

2. AI for Professional Efficiency

a) Task Automation

Task automation is one of the most impactful applications of AI in the professional sphere. Tools like Zapier and Integromat allow you to automate repetitive tasks across different apps and services, such as automatically saving email attachments to cloud storage or notifying your team about new tasks.

For more complex automation needs, Robotic Process Automation (RPA) tools like UiPath and Blue Prism can automate a wide range of tasks, from data entry and report generation to customer service interactions, freeing up time for more strategic work.

b) Decision-Making and Data Analysis

AI's ability to process and analyze large datasets makes it invaluable for decision-making. Tools like Tableau and Power BI turn raw data into interactive visualizations, helping you identify trends and insights that might otherwise go unnoticed.

For more advanced analytics, AI-powered platforms like IBM Watson offer capabilities such as predictive modeling and natural language processing, which can be used to forecast sales, optimize operations, or analyze customer feedback.

c) Communication and Collaboration

Effective communication and collaboration are crucial for professional success, and AI tools can enhance these areas significantly. Grammarly, for instance, uses AI to help you write clearer and more persuasive emails, reports, and presentations, improving your overall communication quality.

AI-powered project management tools like Trello and Asana streamline collaboration by automatically assigning tasks, setting deadlines, and tracking progress, ensuring that projects move forward smoothly even in remote or distributed teams.

d) Customer Relationship Management (CRM)

In sales and customer service, AI-powered CRM tools like Salesforce and HubSpot offer advanced features to help manage customer interactions more effectively. These platforms analyze customer data, predict behaviors, and suggest the best actions to take at each stage of the customer journey.

AI-driven chatbots like Drift and Intercom provide instant customer support, handling inquiries in real-time and allowing your team to focus on more complex issues, improving overall customer satisfaction.

3. Guidelines for Integrating AI into Your Daily Routine

a) Start Small and Scale Up

When integrating AI tools into your daily routine, start with one or two areas where AI can make an immediate impact, such as time management or task automation. Gradually expand your use of AI as you become more comfortable with these tools.

b) Focus on User-Friendly Tools

Not all AI tools require technical expertise. Choose user-friendly tools with intuitive interfaces and clear instructions. Many platforms also offer tutorials and support, making it easier to get started.

c) Keep Data Privacy in Mind

As you start using AI tools, it's important to consider data privacy. Ensure that the tools you choose comply with data protection regulations and offer robust security features. Regularly review the data you share and the tools' privacy policies.

d) Continuously Evaluate and Adjust

AI tools are constantly evolving. Continuously evaluate the tools you're using to ensure they're still meeting your needs, and don't hesitate to switch tools if you find better alternatives.

e) Educate Yourself and Your Team

Take the time to educate yourself and your team on the benefits and limitations of AI. Understanding how these tools work will help you use them more effectively and avoid common pitfalls. Consider offering training sessions or workshops to keep your team up-to-date on the latest AI tools and best practices.

Finally, AI offers a broad range of tools and applications that can significantly enhance both personal and professional efficiency. By integrating AI into your daily routines—whether for content creation, task automation, or decision-making—you can free up time for more meaningful work, improve your productivity, and stay ahead in a competitive world. Remember to start small, choose user-friendly tools, and continuously adapt your approach as you become more familiar with the power of AI.

The Future Ahead

We're stepping into an era that once seemed like a distant dream. Yet, many of these "futuristic" concepts are already being developed or are even in use today. Let's explore what the future with AI might hold, from the immediate changes in our daily lives to the long-term possibilities that could revolutionize our world.

Near-Future AI: The Next Decade

In the coming years, AI will become more integrated into our everyday lives. Here are some changes we're likely to see:

- Smarter Homes: Imagine waking up to a house that knows your schedule. Your AI-powered home system has already adjusted the temperature, started brewing your coffee, and selected your clothes based on your day's activities and the weather forecast. As you eat breakfast, it briefs you on your schedule and the latest news tailored to your interests.

- Advanced Healthcare: AI will play a bigger role in keeping us healthy. Wearable devices will monitor our vital signs 24/7, alerting us and our doctors to potential health issues before they become serious. AI systems will assist doctors in diagnosing diseases more accurately and creating personalized treatment plans based on our genetic makeup and lifestyle.

- Education Revolution: AI tutors will provide personalized learning experiences for students. These AI teachers will adapt to each student's learning style, pace, and interests, ensuring that every child receives an education tailored to their needs. For adults, AI will make lifelong learning easier, offering courses and training programs that fit around our schedules and career goals.

- Autonomous Transportation: Self-driving cars will become common, making our roads safer and our commutes more productive. You'll be able to work, relax, or enjoy entertainment while your AI-driven car takes you to your destination. This technology will extend to trucks, buses, and even flying taxis, changing how we move people and goods.

- Enhanced Customer Service: AI chatbots and virtual assistants will handle most customer service interactions. These AI agents will understand context and emotion, providing human-like support without the wait times. They'll be able to handle complex queries across multiple languages, improving customer satisfaction and reducing costs for businesses.

Mid-Future AI: The Next 25 Years

As AI continues to advance, we'll see more significant changes:

- AI Collaborators in the Workplace: AI won't just automate tasks; it will become an active collaborator in many professions. Lawyers will work with AI partners that can analyze thousands of cases in seconds. Architects will design buildings with AI that can optimize for energy efficiency, cost, and aesthetic appeal.

Scientists will team up with AI to accelerate research and make breakthrough discoveries.

- Personalized Entertainment: AI will create entertainment tailored to individual preferences. It might generate movies or TV shows on the fly, adjusting the plot, characters, and even the visual style based on your reactions and preferences. Virtual reality experiences will become more immersive, with AI creating vast, interactive worlds that respond to your actions and choices.

- Environmental Management: AI systems will play a crucial role in managing our environment. They'll optimize energy grids, reducing waste and increasing the use of renewable sources. AI-driven climate models will provide more accurate predictions, helping us mitigate and adapt to climate change. Smart cities will use AI to manage traffic, reduce pollution, and improve quality of life for residents.

- Advanced Prosthetics and Human Augmentation: AI-powered prosthetics will provide more natural movement and even sense of touch for amputees. Brain-computer interfaces might allow people with paralysis to control devices with their thoughts. We may even see the development of AI-enhanced sensory devices that can extend human capabilities, like infrared vision or ultrasonic hearing.

- AI in Governance: Governments might use AI to help make policy decisions, analyzing vast amounts of data to predict the outcomes of different policies. AI could help design fairer tax systems, optimize public services, and even assist in diplomatic negotiations by analyzing complex geopolitical situations.

Long-Term Future: 50 Years and Beyond

Looking further into the future, the possibilities become more speculative but also more transformative:

- Artificial General Intelligence (AGI): We might develop AI systems that can match or exceed human-level intelligence across a wide range of tasks. These AGIs could solve complex problems in science, medicine, and technology, leading to rapid advancements in these fields. The development of AGI would be a pivotal moment in human history, potentially changing every aspect of our society.

- Space Exploration and Colonization: AI could be crucial in our efforts to explore and potentially colonize other planets. AI systems could manage life support systems on long-term space missions, make split-second decisions in dangerous situations, and even terraform other planets to make them habitable for humans.

- Merging of Human and Artificial Intelligence: Some futurists predict a merging of human and artificial intelligence. This could involve direct interfaces between our brains and AI systems, allowing us to access vast amounts of information instantly or even expand our cognitive abilities. This could lead to a new phase of human evolution, where the line between human and machine intelligence becomes blurred.

- Solving Global Challenges: With advanced AI, we might find solutions to some of our biggest global challenges. AI could help us develop clean, unlimited energy sources, solve world hunger through optimized agriculture and food distribution, or find cures for all known diseases. It might even help us understand and preserve endangered ecosystems or revive extinct species.

- Redefining Work and Purpose: In a world where AI can perform most tasks more efficiently than humans, we may need to redefine the concept of work and find new sources of meaning and purpose. This could lead to a society focused more on creativity, personal growth, and social connections rather than traditional employment.

Miraculous Possibilities

As we push the boundaries of AI technology, scientists and futurists envision some truly extraordinary possibilities that could revolutionize our world:

- Solving Aging: One of the most ambitious goals for AI is to help us understand and potentially reverse the aging process. AI could analyze vast amounts of genetic and biological data to uncover the mechanisms of aging at a cellular level. This could lead to treatments that slow, stop, or even reverse aging, potentially extending human lifespans dramatically. Imagine a world where people routinely live to be 150 or even 200 years old, in bodies that remain youthful and healthy.

- Decoding and Communicating with Animals: AI might help us break the communication barrier with other species. By analyzing animal vocalizations, body language, and brain activity, AI could potentially translate animal thoughts and emotions into human language. This could lead to deeper understanding and cooperation with other species, revolutionizing fields like conservation and potentially changing our entire relationship with the animal kingdom.

- Climate Reversal: While mitigating climate change is crucial, AI might help us go a step further and actually reverse its effects. Advanced AI systems could design and manage large-scale geoengineering projects, such as removing excess CO_2 from the atmosphere or redirecting sunlight to cool the planet. These AI systems could make real-time adjustments based on complex climate models, potentially restoring our planet's climate to pre-industrial levels.

- Unlocking Consciousness: One of the greatest mysteries in science is the nature of consciousness. AI might help us solve this puzzle. By creating increasingly sophisticated models of the brain and mind, AI could help us understand how consciousness emerges. This could lead to breakthroughs in treating mental illnesses, enhancing human cognitive abilities, or even the possibility of transferring consciousness to different substrates.

- Faster-Than-Light Communication: While faster-than-light travel may remain in the realm of science fiction, some scientists speculate that AI could help us achieve faster-than-light communication. By leveraging quantum entanglement and developing advanced AI algorithms, we might be able to instantaneously transmit information across vast distances. This could revolutionize space exploration and potentially allow us to communicate across galaxies.

- Creating New Forms of Matter: AI could help us discover and even create entirely new forms of matter with properties we can barely imagine. By simulating countless atomic and subatomic interactions, AI might uncover new materials that are room-temperature superconductors, have negative mass, or possess other exotic properties. These materials could revolutionize technology, enabling things like lossless energy transmission or gravity manipulation.

- Simulating Universes: With sufficiently advanced AI and computing power, we might be able to simulate entire universes down to the subatomic level. This could allow us to test fundamental theories of physics, explore different laws of nature, or even study the emergence of life and intelligence in these simulated realities. Some philosophers even speculate that such simulations might be indistinguishable from "real" universes, raising profound questions about the nature of our own reality.

- Interstellar Terraforming: AI could be the key to making other planets habitable for humans. By analyzing the composition of distant planets and running complex simulations, AI could design and manage the process of terraforming. This might involve engineering microorganisms to alter a planet's atmosphere, managing complex chemical reactions on a planetary scale, or even adjusting a planet's orbit. With AI, we might transform Mars, Venus, or even more distant exoplanets into new homes for humanity.

These miraculous possibilities represent the extreme edge of our expectations for AI. While they may seem like science fiction today, many of our current AI capabilities would have seemed equally fantastical just a few decades ago. As AI continues to advance, some of these "miracles" might move from the realm of speculation to reality, opening up new frontiers for human knowledge and capability.

It's important to note that these are speculative ideas and not guaranteed outcomes. They represent the most optimistic and ambitious visions for what AI might achieve. Realizing any of these possibilities would require not just advances in AI, but also breakthroughs in other fields of science and technology. However, by imagining these possibilities, we push the boundaries of what we believe is achievable and inspire further innovation and exploration.

Challenges and Considerations

While the future with AI holds exciting possibilities, it also presents significant challenges that we'll need to address:

- Ethical Concerns: As AI becomes more advanced, we'll face complex ethical questions. How do we ensure AI systems make fair and unbiased decisions? What rights should we grant to highly intelligent AI entities? How do we prevent AI from being used for harmful purposes?

- Job Displacement: While AI will create new jobs, it will also automate many existing ones. We'll need to find ways to retrain workers and potentially rethink our economic systems to ensure prosperity is shared widely.

- Privacy and Security: With AI systems processing vast amounts of personal data, ensuring privacy and data security will be crucial. We'll need robust regulations and technological safeguards to protect individual rights in an AI-driven world.

- AI Safety: As AI systems become more powerful, ensuring they remain safe and aligned with human values will be critical. We'll need to solve complex technical problems to make sure AI systems do what we intend and don't cause unintended harm.

- Social and Psychological Impact: The rapid changes brought by AI could have profound effects on human psychology and social structures. We'll need to find ways to adapt to these changes while preserving human connections and mental well-being.

Preparing for the AI Future

Given these possibilities and challenges, how can we prepare for an AI-driven future?

- Education: We need to update our education systems to prepare people for a world where AI is ubiquitous. This means focusing on skills that complement AI, like creativity, emotional intelligence, and complex problem-solving.

- Lifelong Learning: With the rapid pace of AI advancement, continuous learning will be crucial. We should cultivate a mindset of curiosity and adaptability, always ready to learn new skills.

- Ethical Framework: We need to develop robust ethical frameworks for AI development and use. This will require collaboration between technologists, ethicists, policymakers, and the public.

- Inclusive Development: As we shape the future of AI, it's crucial to include diverse perspectives to ensure AI benefits all of humanity, not just a select few.

- Research and Innovation: Continued investment in AI research and innovation will be key to realizing the positive potential of AI while mitigating its risks.

Conclusion

The future with AI holds immense potential to improve our lives and solve global challenges. From smarter homes and personalized healthcare in the near term to the possibility of merging with AI in the distant future, we're on the cusp of transformative changes.

However, this future isn't predetermined. The choices we make today in developing and regulating AI will shape the world of tomorrow. By staying informed, engaging in discussions about AI's role in society, and working to ensure AI is developed responsibly, we can all play a part in creating a future where AI enhances human potential and improves life for everyone.

The journey into the AI future has already begun. It's up to us to guide it in a direction that benefits all of humanity.

Join My Community

https://community.askpndas.com

"The Art of Living".